Whitney

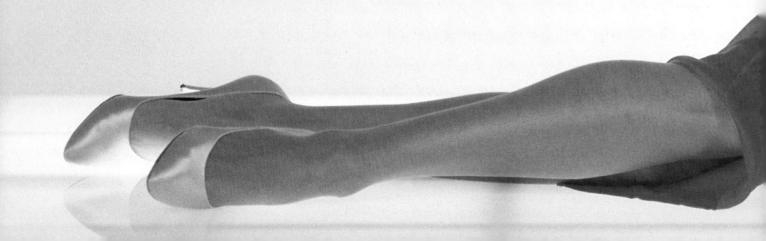

LIFE BOOKS
Managing Editor Robert Sullivan
Director of Photography Barbara Baker Burrows
Creative Director Anke Stohlmann
Deputy Picture Editor Christina Lieberman
Copy Editors Parlan McGaw (Chief),
Don Armstrong, Barbara Gogan
Writer-Reporter Michelle DuPré
Photo Associate Sarah Cates
Consulting Picture Editors Mimi Murphy (Rome),
Tala Skari (Paris)

Editorial Director Stephen Koepp

EDITORIAL OPERATIONS
Richard K. Prue (Director), Brian Fellows
(Manager), Keith Aurelio, Charlotte Coco,
Kevin Hart, Mert Kerimoglu, Rosalie Khan,
Patricia Koh, Marco Lau, Brian Mai,
Po Fung Ng, Rudi Papiri, Robert Pizaro,
Barry Pribula, Clara Renauro, Katy Saunders,
Samantha Schwendaman, Hia Tan,
Vaune Trachtman

TIME HOME ENTERTAINMENT
President Richard Fraiman
Vice President, Business Development & Strategy
Steven Sandonato
Executive Director, Marketing Services Carol Pittard
Executive Director, Retail & Special Sales Tom Mifsud
Director, Bookazine Development & Marketing
Laura Adam
Publishing Director Joy Butts
Finance Director Glenn Buonocore
Assistant General Counsel Helen Wan
Assistant Director, Special Sales Ilene Schreider
Book Production Manager Suzanne Janso
Design & Prepress Manager Anne-Michelle Gallero
Brand Manager Roshni Patel

Special thanks to Christine Austin, Jeremy
Biloon, Jim Childs, Susan Chodakiewicz,
Rose Cirrincione, Lauren Hall Clark,
Jacqueline Fitzgerald, Christine Font,
Jenna Goldberg, Hillary Hirsch, Amy Mangus,
Robert Marasco, Kimberly Marshall,
Amy Migliaccio, Nina Mistry, Dave Rozzelle,
Adriana Tierno, Alex Voznesenskiy, Vanessa Wu

Published by LIFE BOOKS, an imprint of
Time Home Entertainment Inc.
135 West 50th Street
New York, New York 10020

Vol. 12, No. 5 • February 24, 2012

ISBN 10: 1-61893-032-X
ISBN 13: 978-1-61893-032-3
Library of Congress Control Number:
2012933384

"LIFE" is a registered trademark of Time Inc.

We welcome your comments and suggestions
about LIFE Books. Please write to us at:
LIFE Books
Attention: Book Editors
PO Box 11016
Des Moines, IA 50336-1016

If you would like to order any of our hardcover
Collector's Edition books, please call us at:
1-800-327-6388 (Monday through Friday,
7:00 a.m.— 8:00 p.m. or Saturday, 7:00 a.m.—
6:00 p.m. Central Time).

Cover Dirck Halstead
Back cover © Jack Vartoogian/FrontRowPhotos
Page 1 Kevin P. Casey/Polaris
Previous pages Dirck Halstead
These pages Matt Sayles/AP

Whitney

1963–2012

Songbird

She was given a gift and she shared it with the world.
And then came the fall.

PHOTOGRAPHS BY DAVID CORIO

future star was born in Newark, New Jersey, on August 9, 1963, to John Russell Houston Jr. and his wife, Cissy. It couldn't have been predicted yet that this little girl would make it to the top, even though the Houstons' friends would have told you that she sure had the genes. Once she started to sing, with that supernatural voice of hers, this became readily apparent—she had the genes, and she had the pipes—and all she needed, as Judy Garland (playing Esther Blodgett) says to James Mason (as Norman Maine) in the movie *A Star Is Born*, was "just a little luck."

"What kind of luck?" asks Mason.

"Oh, the kind of luck that every girl singer with a band dreams of—one night a big talent scout from a big record company might come in and he'll let me make a record."

"Yes, and then?"

"Well, the record will become No. 1 on the Hit Parade, it'll be played on the jukeboxes all over the country . . . and I'll be made." Garland pauses, and laughs at the implausibility of it all. Then she adds: "End of dream."

"There's only one thing wrong with that," says Mason.

"I know," says Garland. "It won't happen!"

"No, it might happen pretty easily. But the dream isn't big enough."

The dream he refers to would have included all the rest of it, which is life itself. Whitney Elizabeth Houston, as a singer, would get all the luck she needed when record company chieftain Clive Davis heard her at a club in 1983 and then let her make a disc. She would get not only one No. 1 hit, but a veritable slew of them, including an all-time record-setting seven in a row in the 1980s. She would get the adoration of millions of fans around the world. She would get everything a girl singer with a band playing behind her could ask for.

At various turns in the road thereafter, she thought she had been given even more: a successful movie career, a marriage to a man she loved, a wonderful child.

But life can be harsh, and it seems to revel at times in turning triumphs into tragedies, as the stories of others before Whitney—most recently in the popular music sphere those of Michael Jackson and Amy Winehouse—remind us.

Whitney came out of the projects in Newark, soared to the highest heights, but was only 48 when she died in Los Angeles on February 11, 2012.

How did all of this happen so quickly?

Her father was an Army serviceman and entertainment executive. More significantly, her mother was a gospel singer with a beautiful voice for which she had a reputation. Local people knew of Cissy Houston in 1963, and others would soon know more of her. She had already been part of the Drinkard Singers (one of her sisters, in the group and in life, was Lee Drinkard, the mother of the singers Dionne and Dee Dee Warwick). The Drinkards performed regularly at Newark's New Hope Baptist Church and recorded the first gospel album released by a major label, *A Joyful Noise*, in 1958. The year Whitney was born, Cissy formed the Sweet Inspirations, which included Doris Troy as well as Dee Dee and which would (with other members plus always Cissy, until 1969) back such singers as Aretha Franklin, Wilson Pickett, Dusty Springfield, Van Morrison (on "Brown Eyed Girl") and even Elvis Presley. If it isn't enough to say that Dionne and Dee Dee Warwick were Whitney's cousins, and that Cissy Houston was her mother, her godmother was Aretha. And her mom harmonized with the King. That's what is called setting a child up.

In the music world, once she was a star, Whitney's early reputation was as a "good girl." Much earlier, when she was in fact just a little girl, she was precisely that. She didn't grow up in Newark but in a middle-class neighborhood in East Orange, New Jersey, to which her parents moved the family after the 1967 riots in the larger city. Whitney was four at the time of the move, and from East Orange she would, a few years on, attend Mount Saint Dominic Academy, a Catholic girls school in nearby Caldwell. Meantime the family maintained its roots in Newark via the New Hope church, where Whitney learned to play piano and where, at age 11, she made her singing debut with "Guide Me, O Thou Great Jehovah." It can be seen as an irony or a justice or a premonition that her last public singing performance before her death, at a nightclub in L.A. on the Thursday before the Saturday of her death, was of another gospel song, "Jesus Loves Me."

While at Mount Saint Dominic Academy, Whitney met a girl, Robyn Crawford, whom she later described as the sister she never had. They became best pals. We mention this here because it is illustrative of all that would happen in the short life of Whitney Houston, and of the dichotomy in her personality—perhaps of the dichotomy of what came earlier and what came later. Since Whitney would succeed at such a young age, through modeling and then singing, it was natural that her closest friends might constitute her earliest entourage. Robyn was chief among these friends and she stuck, becoming Whitney's longtime assistant. But nothing would be easy in the world of Whitney Houston once she began to gain steam. There would be rumors of lesbianism, and friends and associates would urge her to dump Robyn. Whitney was, rightly, defiant, telling *Rolling Stone* in 1993: "I am so tired of this. I'm really sick of it. People want to know if there's a relationship: Our relationship is that we're friends."

Little of this sturm und drang was on the table at Mount Saint Dominic Academy, where Whitney evolved into a lovely and obviously very talented young woman. Cissy had tutored her in singing, and had urged her to pay attention to Aretha, Dionne, Gladys Knight. "When I heard Aretha," said Whitney later, "I could feel her emotional delivery so clearly. It came from down deep within. That's what I wanted to do." Channeling such urges, she was only 11 when she performed that solo in the junior gospel choir at New Hope Baptist, and she was still in her early teens when she began accompanying her mom in concert. She sang backup on her mother's 1978 solo album, *Think It Over*, and started backing such artists as Chaka Khan, Jermaine Jackson and Lou Rawls as well. At this point, she knew where she was heading in her life—her *career*, as she now started to think of it—and later said that it all felt inevitable: "God gave me a voice to sing with." She also said, long after the dust of celebrity had settled, "When I decided to be a singer, my mother warned me I'd be alone a lot. Basically we all are. Loneliness comes with life."

She was a girl who could sing, and who was preternaturally beautiful. "From the beginning, the camera and I were great friends," she said. "It loves me and I love it." Well before she became famous as an entertainer, she was a successful, nationwide model, one of the first African American girls to appear on the cover of *Seventeen* magazine. Beginning then and through the 1980s and '90s, she was a style and fashion icon, and her look and attitude blurred distinctions. African American girls emulated Whitney, and so did white girls and Hispanic girls and Asian girls and all other girls. Her singularity in this regard would be part of her power going forward: Everyone loved Whitney Houston—her appearance, her attitude, her music—and thereby would she conquer the whole world of popular culture. When she died, headlines referred to her as the Queen of Pop, and this was an obvious reference to the death of Michael Jackson, which had occurred not terribly long before. In the 1980s, she certainly was that, even if the title was not formally bestowed. You might find people on the street back then who didn't buy Whitney Houston albums—you might, if you hunted vigorously—but you couldn't find anyone who didn't like Whitney Houston, think well of her or consider her the biggest thing in the entire world (along with MJ).

Most of these people had heard at least the barebones version of her thoroughly irresistible *Star Is Born*

story: singing in the Baptist church choir, performing with her mother in New York City, being heard by a guy from Arista records—a guy who tells his boss, Clive Davis, that he simply must see this gal—being signed by Clive Davis, the *legendary* Clive Davis, and thereby being ushered into the world of stardom that, by dint of her extraordinary talent, she richly deserves. It truly could have been scripted by Hollywood.

As could have Act Two.

And, more tragically, Act Three.

But to return to Act Two: the years of stardom. She relished those years as she entered into them. Later, she relished them very much less. "You know what I feel? I feel old," she told Anthony DeCurtis for that cover story in *Rolling Stone* in 1993—when she was all of 29 years of age. "For the most part, from the time I was eleven years old, I've been working. I did the nightclubs, I did the modeling, all that stuff . . . It's not as much fun as it used to be. When I first started, I was having a lot of fun. But it ain't fun no more. I enjoy what I do, and it gives me great joy to know other people enjoy what I do. But it's not fun . . . [T]he fun in the business, the excitement, like at the beginning? Gone."

She would live another 19 years feeling more or less the same sad way about her trade, while her daughter became ever more important to her, and her marriage to Bobby Brown, of whom we will learn more in these pages, got better and worse and then very much worse. But back in the day, before she started to feel old, "I was having a lot of fun."

She was indeed. When she began to arrive on some people's radars in the late 1970s, she was something of a pop ingenue à la Lesley Gore or Shelley Fabares of the '60s blended with her true influences (Aretha et al, plus Diana Ross and Gladys Knight et alia), and pointing toward the Madonnas, Rihannas and Adeles yet to come—not to mention the Miley Cyruses and Selena Gomezes. She was the whole package and the

very real deal. She never was much of a dancer (when she became an early generation MTV queen, she did her Whitney shimmy and her supporting crew busted the moves), but she had everything else. Especially that voice, which could go everywhere—up, down or sideways. As a 14-year-old she sang backup on "Life's a Party" by the jazzy Michael Zager Band, and a year later she sang background on Chaka Khan's huge hit "I'm Every Woman" (which would become an even huger hit for Whitney herself a few years on when her version was included on the soundtrack of the film *The Bodyguard*).

The talent was evident to any who witnessed it, and now came that bit of *Star Is Born* luck. In 1980, an A&R exec at Arista Records, Gerry Griffith, had seen her performing with Cissy at the Bottom Line in New York's Greenwich Village. He noticed Whitney—who wouldn't?—but thought her unpolished. "As good as she is, there's still something lacking. She isn't quite ripe yet." Two years later, he saw her again at a different club, 7th Avenue South, and was knocked out. "She was mesmerizing," he told music writer Bud Scoppa. "I couldn't believe she had grown so much in that two-year period. She went from a teenager to a woman. She had a mature look, her voice was more mature, she had obvious star quality. It took no genius to see it—all you had to do was just see her and you knew. I'll never forget, she sang the song 'Tomorrow' from *Annie*, and it was a *showstopper*. After I got up off the floor, I just knew that I had to bring her to the label." But Elektra Records had noticed Whitney too, and was said to be courting. So Griffith implored his boss, Clive Davis, to hear Whitney. Griffith set up a showcase at Top Cat Studio in Manhattan. Davis saw her there, checked her out a second time at a club called Sweetwaters and swooped in with a contract.

In retrospect, Whitney Houston's rise to stardom seems the very definition of meteoric, but there were a few stops and starts in the studio early on. They couldn't find the right material for her, they debated whether to market her to the African American audience or the white audience, whether to push her toward the rhythm and blues charts or the pop, or maybe any and all of the above (which was, of course, the right answer). A duet she recorded with Jermaine Jackson went unreleased when the song, "Don't Look Any Further," was given to another artist. Dennis Edwards, ex of the Temptations, had a No. 2 R&B hit with it, which was lamented in the Houston camp at the time. But Whitney Houston was going places Dennis Edwards could only dream of.

Her first album, *Whitney Houston*, was released in 1985. People in the know—astute culture vultures as well as industry insiders—felt something big was coming. Whitney was already a quantity. Besides the *Seventeen* cover, she had modeled for such magazines as *Young Miss* and *Glamour*, she had appeared in TV ads. She had, as said, sung behind others, and that voice couldn't help but stand out. Robert Christgau, the influential music writer at *The Village Voice*—a kind of curmudgeonly guru among rock critics—said that the song "Memories," on which Houston harmonized with Archie Shepp on an album by a group named Material, was "one of the most gorgeous ballads you've ever heard." That sentiment would be echoed over and over again—applied to a score of Whitney Houston performances—in the years to follow.

A song that would be included on *Whitney Houston*, a duet with Teddy Pendergrass called "Hold Me," was released in 1984 and went Top 5 on the R&B charts. The groundswell began in earnest. In February of '85 the album was released and *Rolling Stone* hailed "one of the most exciting new voices in years." The music world felt it had another Beatles or Michael Jackson on its hands—and this one, a woman. A black woman. "You Give Good Love" was released as a single and went to No. 3. "Saving All My Love for You" was Houston's first No. 1 single in both the United States and the United Kingdom. "How Will I Know" went to No. 1 on the *Billboard* chart as well. Whitney became an MTV fixture in a period when that meant something, and the album just churned on—like Jackson's *Thriller* had. "Greatest Love of All" stayed

in first place for three weeks, and in 1986, *Whitney Houston* topped the album charts for 14 weeks and became the best-selling disc of the year.

"Were you surprised that the first album got so large?" Anthony DeCurtis asked Houston in 1993.

"You know, it gets to the point where the first couple of million you go, 'Oh, thank you, Jesus!'" Houston responded, then laughed. "I mean, let's face it, you make a record, you want people to buy your record—period. Anybody who tells you 'I'm makin' a record 'cause I want to be creative' is a [expletive] liar. They want to sell records. As it went on—and it went on—I took a very humble attitude. I was not going to say, 'Hey, I sold 13 million records—check that [expletive] out.' My mother always told me, 'Before the fall goeth pride.'"

(By the way, the 13 million was just U.S. sales; the record moved 25 million units worldwide, and the Greatest Love World Tour was a sold-out affair.)

So looking back, seven years after the tsunami, Houston saw her younger self as a still-grounded 22-year-old woman. What others were seeing in that young woman in 1985–86 was a unique, altogether extraordinary talent. She could take a ballad and do things with it that no one else could. (Years later, the standard of success on the various reality TV musical shows would be what a contestant could possibly do with "a Whitney Houston song.") It was very difficult, the cognoscenti knew. There were the bass lines to be sung, and then Whitney could fly up to that ravishing falsetto. She was beautiful to boot, but it was mostly about the singing.

A funny phone call regarding one of the biggest hit songs of all time, Whitney's version of Dolly Parton's "I Will Always Love You":

Dolly tells Whitney, "I'm just so honored that you did my song. I just don't know what to tell you, girl."

And then Whitney says humbly, "Well, Dolly, you wrote a beautiful song."

And then Dolly says, "Yeah, but it never did that well for me. It did well for you because you put all that stuff into it."

All that stuff. Whitney Houston could put all that stuff into a song like no one else before or since.

The Grammys and American Music Awards began to rain down, of course (she won seven AMAs in 1986 and '87); the money began to pour in. This was all good. The public looked at lovely, charming, mega-talented Whitney Houston in 1986 and thought: If anyone can handle this kind of celebrity, this young woman can. She's . . . Well, she's a "good girl."

She had opened the door for others. Janet Jackson's and Anita Baker's careers owed a sizable debt to Whitney Houston back in the day, and so do, today, those of Rihanna and Beyoncé. This is not to denigrate such as Whitney's godmother, Aretha, or Diana Ross, but suddenly, in 1986, for a black woman to be the biggest thing on the planet was more than okay. It was fine. For a time there, as we have said, Michael Jackson and Whitney Houston really were the undisputed King and Queen of Pop.

Consider, all these years later: She would eventually sell more than 170 million albums, singles and videos. She would become the most-awarded female entertainer of all time, with 415 prizes, including two Emmys, six Grammys, 30 *Billboard* Music Awards, 22 AMAs. We pause here to cite these statistics because, while children of the 1980s and '90s well remember what Whitney meant to them—how she supplied the soundtrack of their lives and the songs for their weddings—others might have forgotten just how big she was, before the fall.

The fall was still distant in 1987 when her second album, *Whitney*, was released. Not yet 25, she was in fine form and voice, and she now had a second disc that set records (first album by a female artist to debut at No. 1 on the *Billboard* chart, and first album by any entertainer to enter the charts at No. 1 in both the U.S. and U.K.) and that effortlessly and ceaselessly threw off No. 1 hits: "I Wanna Dance With Somebody (Who Loves Me)," "Didn't We Almost Have It All," "So Emotional," "Where Do Broken Hearts Go." The Beatles and the Bee Gees had each had six consecutive chart-toppers in their careers, and now, after the gold rush of singles from Houston's first two albums was finally tapped out, they found themselves tied for second place. Like those acts and her contemporaries Michael Jackson and Madonna, Whitney Houston was a global, not just a national, phenomenon, and as she flew off on another world tour she did so with justifiable confidence.

That was something she possessed in deep quantity: self-confidence. It has been said that when she was a little girl singing Aretha Franklin songs while holding the handle of a vacuum cleaner as if it were a microphone, she imagined the setting not as it was— the basement of the family home—but as Madison Square Garden. And she was dead serious when she said that that was not only her destination but her due. When she was in her teens, she knew she was going to be a star singer (everyone was telling her so) and she chafed when her mom and dad told her: Not yet. The Reverend DeForest "Buster" Soaries Jr., who has known the Houston family for 40 years, remembered in an essay for CNN "a very anxious, very animated, teenaged Whitney leaning over a table at a McDonald's in East Orange, New Jersey. She was frustrated by, but cooperative with, her parents' unwillingness to allow her professional music career to commence too quickly. She began naming the artists whose careers were rising and who she knew she could match vocally."

So this must have felt good to such a young woman, age 24: She had not only matched all others in the pro singing game, she had beaten them. At the 30th Grammy Awards in 1988, she won her second Best Female Pop Vocal Performance trophy. In 1991 she sang the national anthem at the Super Bowl in a rendition that is today remembered as perhaps the best ever, and that at the time, when America was freshly engaged in the first Iraq War, earned half a million as a recording for the Red Cross. (It climbed the charts again when re-released after 9/11, and raised more money for the victims of that tragedy.)

She was, at the dawn of the '90s, the biggest thing in the world.

The music world, anyway.

What other worlds might she now conquer?

When you are young, talented, wildly popular and a world-class beauty, Hollywood comes calling—if not eventually, then sooner than that. Houston had had overtures, certainly—proposed projects with Robert De Niro, Spike Lee—and she was mulling options. She felt she might sidle in, but then came the script for *The Bodyguard*. "I wanted to do some acting, but I mean I never thought I'd be costarring with Kevin Costner!" she told *Rolling Stone*. "I thought 'I'll just get a little part somewhere, and I'll work my way up.' And all of a sudden I get this script, and I said: 'I don't know. This is kind of . . . big.' So I was scared. It took me two years to decide to do it. I kind of waited too long for Kevin. I think it got on his nerves. He called one day and said, 'Listen, are you going to do this movie with me or not?' I told him about my fears. I said: 'I'm afraid. I don't want to go out there and fall.' And he said: 'I promise you I will not let you fall. I will help you.' And he did."

He did, all the way to one of the biggest hits of 1992: over $121 million at the U.S. box office and $410 million worldwide (second that year only to Disney's *Aladdin*). In the film, Houston plays a singer who falls in love with the man who's been hired to protect her from a stalker. (It's perhaps interesting that when Lawrence Kasdan wrote the screenplay in the 1970s, he had Diana Ross in mind for the Houston role, and Steve McQueen in the Costner part.) The film was, in a way, the cinematic equivalent of a Whitney Houston hit song: It certainly didn't wow all the critics and it was flagrantly romantic—but it touched the hearts of millions.

As did its accompanying music. The soundtrack album was unstoppable (it sold over a million copies in one week during the Christmas season of '92, and no album had ever done that in seven days). It was spearheaded by that earlier mentioned version of Dolly Parton's 1974 ballad "I Will Always Love You." The single stayed at No. 1 for a then record 14 weeks and remains the largest-selling record ever by a female artist.

The Bodyguard was, meanwhile, quietly ground-breaking. The director of the film and his lead actors never worried about (or nodded to) the fact that Costner was white, Houston black. The marketers did worry, and in some advertising they obscured Houston's face. As crazy as that seems—to hide the face of one of the most famous people in the world!—it proved as silly as it was crazy. "People loved this movie," Houston told *Rolling Stone* in 1993. "The critics dogged it, but people loved it. They weren't looking at a black person and a white person, they were looking at two people having a relationship."

Houston was the ultimate crossover star. After her second film, *Waiting to Exhale*, was a critical and commercial triumph, she was paid $10 million for her third, *The Preacher's Wife*, opposite Denzel Washington. Later in the 1990s she would not only act in but produce the Disney TV version of *Cinderella*. She played the Fairy Godmother and Brandy was the princess-in-waiting. All of this appealed equally to blacks and whites.

But along the way her music was, as she might have put it, "dogged" by some on the more cutting edge of the African American community. When she was a nominee for an award at the 1989 Soul Train Awards, she was booed by a few in the audience. She later responded defensively: "If you're gonna have a long career, there's a certain way to do it, and I did it that way. I'm not ashamed of it."

If those fans saw a lack of street cred in Houston—

if they perceived her as archaic, shying from the New Jack Swing that was the vogue of the day—they could never have guessed that they were present on the very night that Whitney Houston met a guy who, down the road, would be a big factor in major changes in her image and in her life.

They were there, when Whitney met Bobby.

Search as you might, you cannot find the name Bobby Brown unaffiliated with the phrase "bad boy"—and this isn't entirely due to the eternal attraction of alliteration. There's rap involved, but also a real rap sheet.

When he comes on the scene with the R&B boy band New Edition in the 1980s (they had formed in 1978), he begins to gain his reputation; in fact, he's kicked out of the group for behavioral problems in 1986. Three years later he is flying solo, and he meets the legendary Whitney Houston at the Soul Train Awards. She is intrigued by this energetic, charismatic man five years her junior, and subsequently she invites him to a party. He attends, and they hit it off.

That's how it starts. Earlier in the 1980s, the gossip columns had linked Houston with football star Randall Cunningham and with Eddie Murphy, but this tryst with Bobby Brown is as compelling as it is baffling, and the tabloids can't get enough of it. Houston and Brown persevere in their relationship despite the glare, then wed on July 18, 1992. On March 4, 1993, Bobbi Kristina Houston Brown, who would be Whitney's only child (she was at the time Brown's fourth), is born.

Houston later said that troubles in their marriage started when she gained ever more massive fame in her movie career; that it would have been difficult for any man to handle that. Brown said they separated for the first of several times only a year into their marriage, and that, yeah, sure, he serially cheated on his wife. Perhaps the most astonishing thing is that the union, which we now know involved episodes of domestic violence and lots of drug use, lasted 14 years. In 2005,

Brown coaxed Houston into appearing on his gruesome Bravo reality TV series, *Being Bobby Brown*, and if Whitney's audience was horrified by the husband's casual denigration of his wife, not to mention his daily dissolution, they were even more saddened to see how precipitous had been the wife's decline. She was an addict, and she looked it. She quit the show after a season, and so it was cancelled: It was of no value without the spectacle. She divorced Brown the following year and was awarded custody of their daughter.

The endgame for Whitney Houston was, as we know, lengthy and awful, and had everything to do with substance abuse. There were memorable days even in this bleak period: emotional sojourns to South Africa and the Middle East, the occasional musical comeback, the career awards. But life itself was in a downward spiral from which she could not escape.

She tried. God knows she tried. As recently as May 2011, she enrolled once again in a rehab program, a latest chapter, said her representative, in her "longstanding recovery process." Her fans took heart when they heard a few months later that she was producing and acting in a remake of the 1976 film *Sparkle*, about a Supremes-type girl group whose leader succumbs to drug addiction. She finished the shoot, and that was a good sign. It is said by those who have seen the rushes to be a very good film. They say that Houston is terrific in it. It will be out in August.

At that time, we will have an opportunity again to reflect on the fantastic career and tumultuous life of Whitney Houston. Four decades ago in the basement of that house in East Orange, New Jersey, she took the handle of that vacuum cleaner in hand and sang in a way scarcely to be believed. She dreamed she was in Madison Square Garden. She dreamed she was a star.

A big dream.

It came true.

But even that dream wasn't big enough.

CHAPTER 1

Nippy

That's what family and friends in New Jersey called her:
She was Cissy Houston's daughter, Nippy.

CISSY AND NIPPY were as close as could be in many ways, and while Cissy purposefully paved the way for her daughter's future career, she wouldn't let her jump too soon. Opposite: As if the at-home influence weren't enough, Cissy's dear friend and sometime employer Aretha Franklin agreed to be the girl's godmother.

WHITNEY HAD many sweet inspirations when growing up, principal among them her mom's group, the Sweet Inspirations. Above, from left, are Cissy, Myrna Smith, Sylvia Shemwell and Estelle Brown during a promotional tour in England in 1968. In this year and the next, while five-year-old Whitney would have been back home, the group traveled far and wide, including Vegas, where they backed Elvis. Whitney's father, John, helped manage Cissy's career and was happy to take care of the children when his wife was on the road. "He changed diapers, cooked, did my hair and dressed me, all the while providing Mom with advice and answers," said Whitney. "He was Mom's support network." Opposite: Cousin Dionne Warwick was 23 years older than Whitney and became one of her main idols; this picture is from approximately the time of Whitney's birth in 1963. A fun fact: The highest charting women singers ever on the *Billboard* list are Aretha, with 73 singles registered, then Dionne and Madonna, with 56 each.

NIPPY WAS BORN in Newark but would remember "home" as the house at 362 Dodd Street in East Orange, New Jersey, to which the family moved when she was four. It was in the basement of this building that she would belt out "R-E-S-P-E-C-T!" at the top of her lungs. There is absolutely no question but that she knew what she wanted, and where she was headed, at a very young age: "Being around people like Aretha Franklin and Gladys Knight, Dionne Warwick and Roberta Flack, all these greats, I was taught to listen and observe. It had a great impact on me as a singer, as a performer, as a musician. Growing up around it, you just can't help it. I identified with it immediately. It was something that was so natural to me that when I started singing, it was almost like speaking."

BETTE MARSHALL/GETTY

JOHN W. FERGUSON/GETTY

WELL, EVERY high school girl jaws endlessly on the phone with friends. (Yes, okay, these days they text.) And every high school girl has posters on her bedroom walls of singing stars. But not every high school girl's pictures feature her cousin (Dionne is at left) and her mother (with whom Whitney was already singing in New York City). At left is Mount Saint Dominic Academy, whose alumnae of the period universally say they fully realized Nippy was destined for greatness.

MEET THE HOUSTONS. Above are Cissy and Nippy, and opposite, bottom, are John and Nippy. At top are, from left, Nippy's older brother Michael; Cissy; Nippy; John; and Nippy's older half-brother, Gary Garland. On the pages immediately following, Nippy grooves circa 1982. "I was the only girl, and I was the baby, so a lot of attention went toward me," Whitney told *Rolling Stone* in 1993. She was then asked if her brothers were protective of her. "Ooooh, uh-huh. Are you kidding? The disadvantage of growing up with two boys is that you can't do anything. If they saw me with a boy, it was like . . . 'Who's that?' I was totally like, 'Oh, God, please, just go away.' The advantage was that I knew all the raps." Here, she laughed, then continued. "I knew all the [expletive] that guys could lay on you from A to Z. I got to hear how guys talk about girls."

AFTER WHITNEY started singing in church, and then in clubs with her mother, word got around—and quickly. Reverend DeForest B. Soaries Jr., reminiscing in an essay for CNN after Whitney's death, recalled a particular choir rehearsal: "We realized someone would have to sing the lead part of the Hawkins' hit song 'Changed.' I turned to the choir director, who was a musician for Cissy Houston and the New Hope Baptist Church of Newark, and asked, 'Where's Nippy?'" Nippy was found, and: "By the time Whitney finished singing the song, the rehearsal had completely *changed*—dismantled and turned into a kind of 'praisefest' and revival service. The child had invoked a level of divine inspiration that involved the kind of joyous tears and emotional shouts that were characteristic of the black religious experience. Not only did Whitney's singing completely transform the atmosphere, but it was clear to everyone in that rehearsal that they were in the presence of an unusual talent and that they were eyewitnesses to a superstar taxiing on the runway of success and fame."

THESE THREE PHOTOGRAPHS show Whitney singing, solo and with her mother, in Newark in 1982 and '83. The picture on the pages immediately following shows her hamming it up in the same period during her mother's recording session in Newark. By now, Whitney is champing at the bit, and Cissy and John are reining her in: "Not so fast, girl." But if Cissy is urging caution and enforcing her counsel, she is also building the bridge. She brings Nippy along to nightclubs as a backup singer, and in fact one of the first places Clive Davis hears Whitney sing is at Sweetwaters, on the Upper West Side of Manhattan, where Cissy is quite purposefully showcasing her daughter. She knows, without any bitterness, that Whitney is destined for a vastly different kind of career than the one she has enjoyed.

SAM EMERSON/POLARIS (2)

GOING PRO: It's 1984, and starting to happen. (In Whitney's mind, it's *finally* starting to happen.) Above, she's at the piano, and opposite she rehearses with Jermaine Jackson before their guest appearance on the CBS soap opera *As the World Turns.* On the pages following they are in the studio recording, but their first efforts at a hit single are frustrated when their song is given to another singer, and their version goes unreleased. For Whitney, liftoff is on hold . . . but not for long.

AS WE NOW KNOW, she would hardly need a second career, but she could have had one. Well, actually, she *did* have one: as one of the world's most sought-after movie stars. But earlier, there was modeling. She signed with the famous Wilhelmina agency in New York City and appeared not only on the cover of *Seventeen* magazine but on *Glamour*'s too. Quite quickly, however, she was a bit too busy to fit the photo shoots in. She had this singing she had to do.

CHAPTER 2

Superstar

From the first note she sang after Clive Davis introduced her, she was connected to her people. From the first note they heard, they loved her.

presented to **whitney houston**
for sales in excess of **100.000** copies
in holland
august 1986

SAM EMERSON/POLARIS

CONDE NAST ARCHIVE/CORBIS

AS WHITNEY enters the game and then takes her first victory laps, the two people by her side are her mother and Arista Records founder and chief executive Clive Davis. On the pages immediately previous, Davis presents her in 1984—after he has signed her to his label but before there is any record to be released. Opposite: Chump change for her first album, as Whitney charmingly accepts an award for selling more than 100,000 copies in Holland. Above: The accolades start to pour in, and the Houston mère et fille are there to accept at the 1987 American Music Awards (top) and then, greeted by Davis, at the same year's Grammys.

ON OCTOBER 11, 1986, Whitney feels the love in Amsterdam during the Greatest Love World Tour. It would never be better than this: Her record was red hot, her concerts were thrilling, she was singing beautifully, her life was relatively uncomplicated—a lot less complicated than it would become, certainly, and with people older and wiser than her ready to help at a moment's notice. Just by the way: The biggest song of the year in the U.S. was by "Dionne and Friends," which was fronted by Whitney's cousin. Their ballad, "That's What Friends Are For," raised millions for AIDS research. It was just the kind of effort that Whitney would be approached for, or would initiate, in the years ahead.

PETER MAZEL/SUNSHINE/ZUMA

The Boston Herald
SAY 'NO' TO DRUGS!
GOVERNOR'S ALLIANCE

OPPOSITE: The terrible irony of this picture from 1986 needs no comment. Above: Jermaine Jackson, Valerie Simpson, Clive Davis, Houston and Nickolas Ashford get together at a 1980s Grammy after-party, as do Whitney and Dionne on the same evening. Nick Ashford, the longtime songwriting and singing partner of his wife, Valerie Simpson, predeceased Houston by just a few months; he was 70 years old.

TO THE MANNER BORN, so to speak, Whitney was always at home in the recording studio, as here with a plush friend in 1987. Nevertheless, the success of her music was entirely built on the voice, not on bells and whistles added in the production process. Clive Davis made sure he lined up the best and most compatible producers for every song (that's the veteran Narada Michael Walden above at right), but their job was always the same: to showcase the voice that had been bequeathed to Whitney by Cissy (opposite)—and, many would say, by God.

ABOVE: On March 2, 1988, Whitney is clearly happy at Radio City Music Hall in New York City, having been awarded the Best Female Pop Vocal Performance Grammy. But despite some pretty nifty videos, she would never win an award for her dancing. Opposite: In concert in Rotterdam in 1988.

WHITNEY AND HER PARENTS, seen during the later 1980s on these pages, were committed to family and to God. When there is talk of the influences on Whitney, Cissy is often cited, but John, too, who died in 2003, played a crucial role. Reverend DeForest B. Soaries Jr. remembers that John Houston "was a part of a political movement that produced Newark, New Jersey's first African American mayor in 1970, Kenneth Gibson. [Whitney] inherited from both of her parents a keen but little known interest in, and passion for, issues, projects and people that improved the plight of blacks and other disadvantaged populations. This is why she was so honored to meet and develop a relationship with South African leader Nelson Mandela. Whenever we spoke over the years, Whitney always took an interest in discussing whatever community project I was working on and she herself was determined to make a difference in people's lives."

TO FOLLOW ON from Reverend Soaries's comments on the previous page: Whitney was indeed honored to meet and develop a relationship with South African leader Nelson Mandela. Here, in 1986, performing at the Nelson Mandela Freedom Festival at Clapham Common in London, she has not yet met him, as he is still imprisoned in South Africa. Houston would return in 1988 for a Mandela 70th birthday tribute at Wembley Stadium that was broadcast to 67 countries and seen by perhaps 600 million people worldwide. It is thought by many that the activism in London by entertainers greatly ratcheted up the pressure on the South African government and led to Mandela's being released sooner than he might have been. He was freed in 1990 after 27 and a half years in prison. On page 76 of our book we will visit with him again—now as the president of his country.

GIDEON MENDEL/CORBIS

POLARIS

THEY ABSOLUTELY OWNED the '80s. Sure, Madonna laid claim to a share, and so did U2, but Michael Jackson and Whitney Houston were the King and Queen of . . . well, yes, Pop. And today it is awful to contemplate what has happened—and, if one listens to Houston's 2009 interview with Oprah Winfrey after Jackson had died, it is eerie. "Mike and I were very close," Houston said. "No one have I ever met quite like that young man." Saying she found Jackson's death "devastating," Houston took herself back to the moment: "I thought, 'This can't be true. This can't be true.' I knew he was on painkillers at one time. I didn't know how far and how deep it was." Or might she have suspected? She went on to recall taping Jackson's 30th Anniversary Celebration in 2001, when both singers were in trouble with substance abuse and obviously frail. "I was getting scared. [I was] looking at myself going, 'No, I don't want to be like this. This can't happen. Not both of us.'" Winfrey asked her: "Was he a mirror for you?" Houston answered, "In some ways, yes. I didn't want to go down that road."

RON FREHM/AP

CHAPTER 3

Diva

Now on top, Whitney begins to swing
and sway. At times it seems she doesn't know
which way she truly wants to go.

IT ONCE WAS THOUGHT that cousin Dionne might help Whitney along. Now, in April of 1990 (opposite), Whitney can help Dionne as she boosts the charitable effort "That's What Friends Are For" during a CBS TV special that her cousin has spearheaded. On this page, above, is a very special moment. Many people feel that there have never been better pre-game performances than Ray Charles singing "America the Beautiful" at the Leonard-Duran boxing match and Whitney Houston's 1991 Super Bowl rendition of "The Star Spangled Banner." It truly was wonderful—chilling, spine-tingling, fully felt—and thanks to the Internet, it can still be summoned. It will live on forever.

EVERYONE WANTS WHITNEY! At top, she is performing at the Arena Leipzig in Germany during one of several comeback tours. Above, she sings with Stevie Wonder for a VH-1 "Divas Duets" benefit concert. Opposite, she lets the kids know that she's still cool during Nickelodeon's Kids' Choice Awards (that's Mark Curry who's been slimed). On the following pages: A million watts of vocalese, as Mariah Carey and Whitney sing "When You Believe" for the soundtrack of Disney's *The Prince of Egypt* movie in 1998.

A GIANT AMONG GIANTS: Whitney Houston was, in the 1990s and in the new millennium, one of the most famous people in the world. She could hobnob on an equal footing with such as Luciano Pavarotti (top) and Tony Bennett (above), but more importantly she could travel to South Africa in 1994, give three concerts and meet her lifelong hero, Nelson Mandela (right).

SHE IS REMEMBERED as a singer, but at one point, she was Hollywood's most sought-after actress. On these pages, her triumphs: She falls in love with Kevin Costner in *The Bodyguard* (top), and skates with Denzel Washington in *The Preacher's Wife* (above); she schmoozes with her friends in *Waiting to Exhale* (opposite, top) and offers advice to Brandy's Cinderella (bottom).

WARNER BROTHERS/EVERETT

PHOTO 12/POLARIS

BUENA VISTA PICTURES/EVERETT

MARY EVANS/RONALD GRANT/EVERETT

THE SUBJECT "Whitney and Bobby" became magazine, tabloid and reality TV fodder in America, and the unfortunate aspect of that is that it refutes any notion of family. Sure, of course they were irresponsible—hardly the best parents. But it is to be assumed they were in love, and loved their daughter. Above is this curiously put-together couple in 1994. Opposite are Whitney and daughter Bobbi in 1993. On the following pages we have a photograph of another one of Whitney's close friends in this period, boxing champion and resolute ne'er-do-well Mike Tyson, who further complicated Whitney's image. It might be something of a credit that Whitney didn't care what others said. She had her friends, and she stood by them. Whether or not she was dragged down by them is a societal judgment to be rendered by others.

LORI SHEPLER/LA TIMES/POLARIS

GARY GERSHOFF/RETNA

GINA FERAZZI/LA TIMES/POLARIS

TOM DONOHUE/POLARIS

BY NOW, she was in trouble, but she still could be on her game. At top, she and Denzel Washington cohost the NAACP Image Awards in Pasadena, California. Just below that, she presents Muhammad Ali with the Arthur Ashe Courage Award at *GQ* magazine's Men of the Year awards. Above, she and Clive Davis preside at a pre-Grammy gala honoring David Geffen at the Beverly Hilton (where, finally, she would perish). Right: At the World Music Awards in Las Vegas, she acknowledges those who love her still.

PAUL SMITH/FEATUREFLASH/POLARIS

MITCHELL GERBER/CORBIS

RICKI ROSEN/SABA/CORBIS

MOSHE SHAI/POLARIS

AN EPISODE in an otherwise troubled time that clearly—*clearly*—meant something to her: In 2003, Whitney and her family went to the Holy Land. She said she was seeking inspiration for her upcoming Christmas album (which would be a lovely album indeed). Upon arriving in Israel, Whitney said she had never felt so at home. In Jerusalem, she, Bobby and daughter Bobbi visited the Old City, and at one point Whitney took a spiritual bath. In her later years—her last years—Whitney sought out things important to her, but she did not like where she was headed. This is not abnormal with people who are in trouble. On the following pages: Whitney, now with many years behind her, cuddles with her mother.

KEVIN UNGER/ZUMA

THERE IS A PHRASE: She lost it all. Few have lost as much as Whitney Houston did, because she had gained such a quantity. She was on top of the world in many, many ways. Clockwise from top left: She and Bobby Brown take part in the infamous Diane Sawyer interview in 2002 in which Whitney admits there might be drugs around but petulantly denies using crack; Houston arrives at the Lamoreaux Justice Center in Orange, New Jersey, to file a petition against Brown; the couple's New Jersey mansion, featured prominently in the egregious *Being Bobby Brown,* is for sale for $1.75 million as we go to press; their house in the exclusive gated Country Club of the South in Alpharetta, Georgia, has been sold; this other house is part of the New Jersey property; a grand piano is moved to auction because Houston has failed to pay storage fees. Opposite: And yet, she could still sing, on her better nights, and she could conjure memories for us all when we heard that voice. And maybe she conjured memories for herself as well.

CHAPTER 4

Coda

Around the world, candles were lit and memories rekindled—as seen here in Leimert Park in Los Angeles. Her troubles were mourned. Her brilliance was remembered.

IT WAS OF COURSE very strange that Whitney Houston died in Los Angeles only hours before she was to attend Clive Davis's pre-Grammy weekend party. The music world—and all fans of music, everywhere—focused on something bigger than even Adele's rightful coronation, as Davis shed tears for the woman he had so supported. On the Sunday night after the Saturday tragedy, Jennifer Hudson, a favorite of Whitney's, sang "I Will Always Love You." Battling her own emotions, Hudson performed wonderfully. Hers might be the second best rendition ever.

MARIO ANZUONI/REUTERS

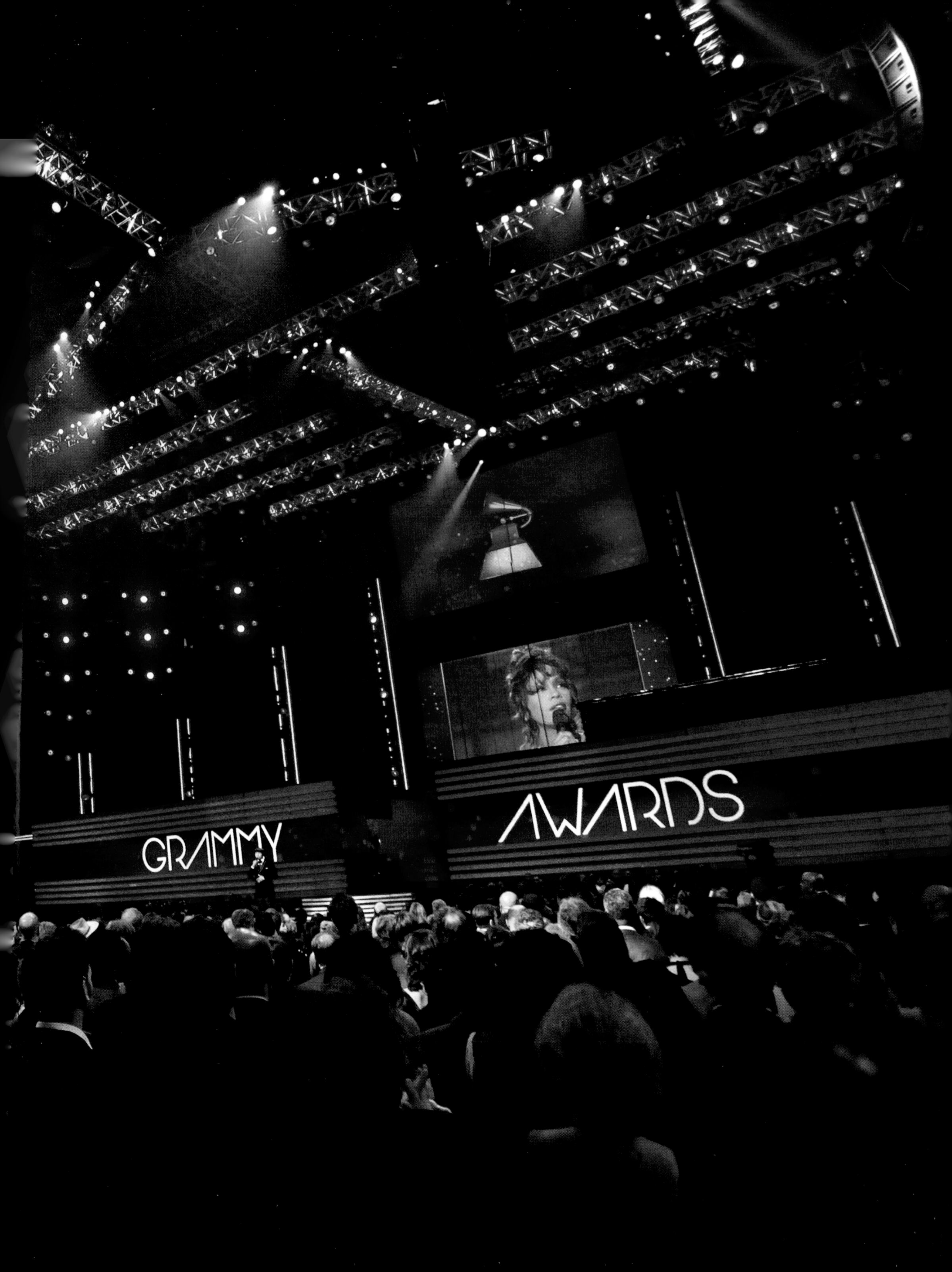
GRAMMY
AWARDS

MATT SAYLES/AP

Whitney Elizabeth Houston

1963–2012